Coming Down the

A Book of Poetry
By Carlton B Reid III

Holy Mountains

Holy mountains dance without moving.

They dance with the crevice, the jagged
Jut of some stone extending into the sky,
The rhythm of the lines,
The curves of the mountain.
Yes, this mountain is holy.

The goats climb to the rhythm since there's
No other way to climb except with the mountain's rhythm.

Who can sense the mountain's rhythm?

Can God?

He created the mountain,
and Moses had to dance down the mountain,
Twisting with the path, skipping over cracks.

Yes, David danced without a mountain.
He danced with God as his mountain.

Long gone are the days where people
Worship on mountains.

Now they worship in Spirit and truth.
They dance with the mountain—
The mountain near their heart,
The Spirit of God.

Climbing the Stairs

I won't let pain define me.
Time will kneel before my
Quickened mortal flesh.

Yes, just like Old Elijah,
With his grey beard,
I'll outrun a chariot
Pulled by warhorses.

The horses will whinny,
They'll neigh, and pay
Their respects to the old
Man running past their
Strong bodies.

Yes, like Elijah, I won't
Ride a chariot until it's
My time—the time to die.
God will send a chariot to
Raise me from the grave.

I'll ride outside my decaying
Body. I'll climb, climb, climb!
Into the sky. The sky won't know
what hit it. It'll say, "Was it a plane?
Was it a bomb? Was it God?"

And I'll yell, "You're wrong!
I'm done with suffering! I'm done
With pain. I'm going to heaven where
Each day I play. I'll dance with the lion.
I'll play with the Lamb. I'll kiss His soft

Garment and howl to the moon."

Yes, if an old wolf like me can get there,
Why can't you?

Comorbidities

I developed the habit at a young
Age. When I was eight,
I followed the paper bag with
My eyes. My mother, Wanda, passed
The chicken with her hands.
I opened the cardboard box,
And was nervous.
WOULD IT TASTE GOOD?

This question killed my mother.
My mother, Wanda, passed
The chicken to me.

At thirty,
I ate the wing of fried
Chicken while feeling bad.
It felt wrong to eat chicken
After her passing.
It felt wrong to eat,
When she ate herself to death,
With diabetes, cholesterol, and
A stroke.

That was the last day I ate fast food.
That was the first day I cried for my mother.

The Cause of Life

The cause of life is complex,
Yet simple.

Two Teenagers,
One room,
One quick
Decision.

A Goat is Far Up the Mountain

Far up the mountain where
The snow melts,
I send my prayers with a loud
Belt.

A belting of the lungs, a throttle
Of the throat.

The throat melts
Snow for water.

The lungs breathed hard
Then softer.

How long will the skies grow cloudy?
How long will my spirit wait?
How long will the apples fail to grow?
How long 'til I feel no pain?

U.S. Ships in 2020

Body in the barrel!
Body in the barrel!

A humble man has died!
A black man has died!

Body in the barrel!
Body in the barrel!

The murderers can't hide!
The murderers can't hide!

Body in the barrel!
Body in the barrel!

Time to say goodbye,

To racism,

I say,

"Farewell."

Racism like Rain

How long until hate leaves
This country?

How long until sun rays?

The ebb and flow of chaos.

The distilling of pain.

How long until hate leaves
This country?

How long until sun rays?

Racism like rain.

Time smells like dandelions

Time smells like dandelions.
I smell like mud dried by the sun.
God smells like the flood.
Time smells like dandelions.

How long until the fire?

Fire burns for a reason.
Sometimes due to seasons.
Water loves to expand.
Always for one reason.
How long until the fire?
How long until the flood?
How long until the canopy
of heaven crumbles
And Jesus comes again.

Black

Black child, black child,
Come sing of the promise—

God promised the Israelites,
God promised our parents,
God promised our children,
God promised our grandparents,

When they sang spirituals,
When they first heard of you
From the Father's lips, promises
Of justice, from his blessed word.
"More than conquerors!" He said.
"More than conquerors!" He bled.
"More than conquerors!" He cried,
"It is finished." Then died,
And rose again.

The promise is for taking
Through faith, no ounce of doubting,
He came to free our souls
And answer faith
Through
Our
Action.

When the Revolution Calls

When the revolution calls,
I'll go.
When the revolution calls,
I'll vote.

Long down under
the trenches,
Lay the earthworms,
Swimming in the dirt.

They see every lie
a politician makes.
They see every lie
the president makes.

And they eat it. Lies
Are buried for a reason,
Yet the wise assemble
The remnants of each
Lie, the worm feces,
And they discover
The truth.

Broken like a mad dog

I've been broken like a mad dog.
I foam at the mouth, and I howl.

I've been broken like a mad dog,
Rolling in the pieces of my life.

Put the egg back together! Put the egg back together!

The egg had a problem.
The age of it all.
The egg had a problem.
The cracks, the missing pieces.

No one wanted the egg to work,
It seemed,
Except for the woman,
But not the man.

Time is like a Chicken, Not a Bear

Time is not a chicken, nor is it a bear,
But it is like a chicken, but not like the bear.
Who decided to make time like a chicken,
So elusive and difficult to pinpoint.
Is everything the present?
Does the present even exist?

Time for a Renegade

"Time for a renegade!"
They chanted.
"Rene-rene-renegade!"
"Rene-rene-renegade!"
"Why does nobody
Stop and take the time
To pray?"

Rhymes are cheesy, and
So is repetition.
But the time for waiting has ended,
And the time for praying
Has started.

Actions that smell like smoke

That man's actions smell like smoke.
It's not so much that his hands smell.
It's not so much that he smokes a thing.
It's just that... That man's actions smell
Like smoke.

I told him, and he paused. The gesture of
His hands and the contour of his mind.
I could not see his mind, but I could sense
The thoughts shifting like smoke, thick
Then thin, there then gone, yet not really
Gone. His thoughts were elusive, elusively
Profound, profoundly
Elusive.
Profound a man was he.
He blinked his eyes like the wings of a
Butterfly. He winked with his teeth, and
He said,
"You got a smart head kid,
But the best thing about being silent
Is that people assume you're wise
When you're really not."

The best time to cry, the best time to die.

The best time to die is when you're dead.
The best time to cry is not the same.
It's not "acceptable" to cry in front of people.
It's not "acceptable" to die with no one there.
It's not "acceptable" to voice a true opinion.
It's not "acceptable" to squash a valid lie.
The best time to cry is when you're crying.
The best time to die is when you die.

I got a firefly.

Fireflies are precious hopes,
Flickering off and on, and
They tend to stay precious only
For children.

Fireflies are precious hopes,
Flickering on and off, and
Adults need to search instead
Of remembering fondly.

They need to go and catch
Their hopes that fly,
Like a fire in the sky.

The time of perfect eating

The time of perfect eating comes
From the gut.
A rumble of the tummy and squeal
Of hunger
Are necessary to avoid killing oneself
With food in
America.

Some know in part

Some know in part,
While some know close to nothing.
They cling to the void where knowledge
Dies.

Some know in part,
While some know close to nothing.

Eating a popsicle

Eating a popsicle never
Calmed my stomach,
But it
felt so good to run ice
Across my tongue, like
when the saxophone
Played. Smooth yet
Biting, cool yet
Dying to the sun and
The heat of my mouth.
The tongue is a wildfire,
And even without any words
Being spoken, I burn.

Soft like a tiger face.

I always imagined tiger faces
Would feel soft, with their large
Manes, not quite like a lion's, but
Tiger manes always seemed smoother
Than some
Or most for that matter.
Handsome.
I'll approach the tiger with my hand
Using a computer screen, but I know
He's too dangerous to touch and meet
In person.
Like how a lot of men are too dangerous
For women to meet alone in person, or how
Some animals are just too dangerous to touch.
Much like a lion
Or tiger.

When the tiger cries

When the tiger cries will be a day
Of great rejoicing,
For the predator
Has repented;
although,
Restitution
Is in the natural order.

The Leaf

The lonely leaf, the first
Out of a long line of firsts,
Was the first to fall from the tree.

He wandered. He cried. As the wind,
Never let him die
In peace.

The essence of who he was,
And the meaning behind his love,
Landed with a delicate touch

On the slow
River, who didn't know
Care much for a dying leaf.

Some people prefer dandelions

I prefer dandelions.
The fancy flowers, the expensive
Power that breeds them. The flourish
From corporate, the ease of purchase,
The corruption that created the thorns...

I prefer dandelions.
I prefer simple people,
not stupid or foolish,
But those who are content with people
For who they are, not who they think
They should be; though, I must admit,
That does not excuse mistakes.

I prefer dandelions.
I prefer them, because I am simple,
Not stupid or foolish,
But I prefer people like myself,
Those with little guile, little deceit—
Those who can thank God for the wind
And trees, those who appreciate nature.

No need for fancy gold or silver,
For dandelions are more precious than gold,
More valuable than silver.

Always a question to be had.

Words never depart from my lips.
That does not mean I always speak
(That would be foolish), but I have words
For every situation and matter. Words meant
To soothe the crying child, words suited to silence
The arrogant with their complex arguments. Yes,
I understand the arguments, but I know that more
Important than an argument is the simple concern of
The common human:

"What will I feed my child?"
"What will I eat for breakfast?"
"How can I keep my house?"

Yes, these concerns are important.
They highlight the complex interests
Of the powerful who ignore the simple
Concerns of the weak, not that they are weak
In character, but that they have less, eat less,
Live in less. This is a concern most common to
Humanity. Who shall answer the call? Who shall
Pick up the cause... The Good Cause!

The Good Cause

The Good Cause is such and only such:
To aid the widow and the orphan and
To not be polluted by a corrupt world,
Such religion is without fault and pure
Before God.

The Good Cause takes the human form
Of Jesus the Christ, the son of God,
For God is love, and Jesus is the expression
Of that love within the bigger equation that says:
Protecting women from being exploited
plus
Aiding the child with no parents
plus
Avoiding corruption from wealth, power, fame,
Equals
Love.

To do so while thinking others more highly than oneself,
To do so while renouncing all claims on profit that corrupts,
To do so while mourning with those who mourn,
To do so while acting on what is noble, true, just, and honest:

These are aspects of
The Good Cause—
A question of metaphysics,
An ethical conversion,
The knowledge of all to come.

A power dynamic

It's hard to name good Christian men
And women, because only God knows
Who truly is a Christian...?
Many will say, "Lord, Lord." But he will say,
"I never knew you."

Many claim to be devout believers, but few
Walk the narrow road, and even those who walk
The narrow road may be denied entry on account
Of the arrogance to say, "I have no sin." For His word
Is not in them.

The answer is a simple power dynamic, between
The weak and God.

One must acknowledge
One is weak and prone to sinning due to many
Weaknesses, and one must acknowledge God is
Jesus, and that God raised Jesus from the dead.
Confusing I know, but that is the hope—the reality
Of things to come. The Faith which millennia of
People waited for, which David waited for, the
Redeemer which Job said surely lives, for Jesus
Redeemed us, and God gave us

Hope.

Seek Others, not myself

I have seen a new message--
The Lord has said through his
Servant: "Seek the good of others,
Not of yourself." This is a troubling
Message to the person focused on self,

For the harvest is plenty, but the workers
Are few. Come down to the sinners and eat
With them, you Christians. But do not eat
Food sacrificed to idols, for their sake, not your
Own. God is flying through the clouds.

God is breaking barriers of sound. Barrier-breaker.
That is his name. He breaks the sound of angels singing
With his voice. He shatters it. He shatters the lies of the devil.
He reaches down from heaven—to the lofty mountaintops to
Touch the hearts of nations. He breaks the shackles of lions.

Jesus has said, "Love me, and Love your neighbor." When others
Ask you to participate in sin, reject the offer for their sake. How
Horrible it would be to allow others to feed you sin, for not only
Do you sin, but most importantly, They sin. Do not question the
Word. But if you do question the Bible, know that he is faithful
And just to forgive us and strengthen our faith. He is patient:
"Ask, and it will be given to you. Seek, and you will find. Knock,
And the door will opened to you."

Walk in the spirit, and you will not satisfy the lusts of the flesh.
Seek the good of others, and you will not satisfy the lusts of the
flesh.
Love your neighbor and you will have fulfilled the whole law.
Seek the good of others, and you will have fulfilled the whole law.

What does good fruit look like? What does the product of a life devoted
To God look like? It is not concerned with the praises of others, for one
Day they love you, and one day, the hate you. They repay mercy with
Judgement and good with evil. "Mercy is greater than judgement."
So, what shall we do? We shall go to the harvest and dance with our
Neighbor who rejoices. We shall go to the harvest and weep with the
Neighbor who mourns. We shall go to the mountains and pray in

The solitude of our closed doors, where no one can hear us. They
Will not be able to know that you are praying.

Your eyes may be open.
Your ears may be listening.
Your body may seem normal.

But, you will be looking for God.
But, you will be listening for God.
But, the heart will be kneeling before God.

Seek the good of others.
Seek not your own benefit.

For when you do, your world will be turned
upside down.

What used to threaten you and cause you fear
Will sleep in the lion's den, after you enter.

What used to worry you, will have its mouth shut,
After you are sentenced to be eating by a multitude of lions.

God is good. He loves you. He made you, and you are His.

Not mere shutting of lions, but the shutting of hell.

Not mere tears of repentance, but the circumcised heart.

Not mere human love for others, but the Agape of God poured through you, His servant and vessel—

A conduit for love.

The Mountain's Face

Who is he that thrashes against the
Mountain's face? Who is he that declares
Himself a superior race? Are not all the
Animals of the field? Are not all the
Wind-pushed grass? Are not most
A reef beaten by pollution? Are most not
The confused, naked in the water?

How can the calm understand groaning?
How can the disturbed know peace?

The reed shaking in the wind knows not where
Distrust will take him, so...
He trusts in that which he cannot "see," and
the God which he knows he "hears." So,

It is for the mountain's face, who
Watches the thrashing man.

How can the calm understand groaning?
How can the disturbed know peace?

So does the mountain watch the man in
pain and say,
"Only for a little while, compared to heaven."

Lightning Source UK Ltd.
Milton Keynes UK
UKHW010641111120
373204UK00001B/138